THE BIOGRAPHY OF DAVE GROHL

TABLE OF CONTENTS

PRESENTATION

Dave Grohl is the previous drummer of Nirvana and current frontman/guitarist/artist for Foo Fighters.

After recording drums on Nirvana's Nevermind collection, he was approached to go along with them as a full-time drummer in 1990 after their past drummer Chad Channing had been terminated during the beginning phases of recording meetings for in Utero (he would later be rehired to record the melodies Oh, the Guilt and Curmudgeon), yet declined to zero in on his music.

The tune "I'm in Love with my Car," from Queen's 1975 Night at the Opera, allegedly motivated him towards a more substantial interest in hard rock and heavy metal music. He likewise respects Black Sabbath bassist Geezer Butler. His number one collections incorporate Black Sabbath's Master of Reality, Fugazi's 13 Songs, and The Stooges' Fun House.

In the mid-1990s, Grohl shaped a gathering called Mission Impossible with Krist Novoselic and Aaron Burckhard. In 1991 they delivered a self-named collection on the Macola Records name. The band was so named on the grounds that it was at first simply intended to be an impermanent venture to record a solitary tune for a gathering collection by different specialists on Seattle's free record name Sub Pop. In any case, because of its individuals concluding that they functioned admirably together subsequent to recording a said tune named "Divine," they chose to keep cooperating and composing more melodies. Subsequent to going through a few names for the band, including "Go," which Grohl detested so much that he promised never to be in a band called Go. They chose the name "Mission Impossible" in the wake of being propelled by a logo with that title on a sewing machine bought from a second-hand shop.

In 1994, Grohl was selected to assist with reproducing drum tracks that had been at first recorded by simple tape for In Utero by Nirvana drummer Kurt Cobain on Pro Tools on the grounds that Cobain had been not able to play them himself convincingly enough for the last blend (Cobain's guitar and vocal tracks were fine). He additionally composed music for two melodies: "Marigold" and "Sodden Vagina." Despite blended sentiments about his exhibition contrasted with Cobain, Grohl was glad for his work and didn't preclude working with the band later on.

In 1995, he played drums on Killing Joke's subsequent self-named collection. Eventually, just two tunes highlighting Grohl were remembered for that record: "This Is a Call" and "I'll Stick Around." different tracks were recorded by a combination of different performers to go with Grohl's vocals, including Krist Novoselic (who had additionally played bass on one channel when standard part Nate Mendel was inaccessible). This acquired him an arrangement with Atlantic Records, which delivered Foo Fighters' introduction collection in 1995.

Albeit this material has been broadly accessible since its delivery, it is still actually unreleased. It isn't known whether Foo Fighters were authoritatively credited as the artists on the collection.

After Nirvana's disbanding, Grohl was selected by Tom Petty to drum in his band for the "She's The One" film soundtrack. A portion of the tunes he recorded with them in the long run displayed on their Greatest Hits collection (Petty once proposed that Grohl join his band, which would've made him an authority part). He additionally recorded drums for two tracks during these meetings; one of these tracks was a revised variant of The Color and the Shape track "Strolling After You," which shows up as an additional track on specific releases of that collection. In 2003 those accounts were delivered under Lee Ving and Freddy Cricien Present: A Tribute to Walking After You.

Grohl has drummed for some groups other than his own, including Paul McCartney's collection Standing Stone (1997) and the X-Ecutioners' "It's

They were going Down" single in 2002. He played drums on one track of the Joey Ramone solo collection Don't Worry About Me in 2002. Grohl likewise contributed drums to the melodies like "Younger Sibling," a Queens of the Stone Age B-side that showed up on their 2000 collection Rated R, Dave Navarro's 2004 independent tune "Oily Love," Death from Above 1979's presentation collection Heads Up in 2003, Mystery Achievement by The Hives in 2000, Nine Inch Nails' Year Zero Remixed EP in 2007, Evanescence's 2011 collection "Vanishing," and the "I Never Came" on their 1998 self-named collection.

Grohl was credited as an author and chief for three Foo Fighters tunes: "Enormous Me," "February Stars," and "Strolling After You." He additionally played drums at Bob Dylan's 50th birthday celebration party in 1997, with Tom Petty and The Heartbreakers. Grohl was helped by Jim Keltner, who played percussion during this Concert. In 2009, Grohl drummed on Slash's presentation solo collection Slash. On July 18, 2009, Grohl performed with Led Zeppelin vocalist Robert Plant at London's O2 Arena as an accolade for Ahmet Ertegün, who had kicked the bucket earlier. In December 2012, Grohl filled in for Zwan's Jimmy Chamberlin at a Smashing Pumpkins show on Republic New York.

In 2014, Grohl drummed a few times with The Rolling Stones at various shows of their 14 On Fire visit through Asia and Australia.

Grohl likewise did a two-day meeting with Infectious Music Band Righteous Fool in the wake of meeting frontman John King by chance at a grill in Venice, CA. Recording drums for four tunes from Righteous Fool's "Melody Inside My Head" collection upgraded Grohl's relationship with Talinda

Bennington (Linkin Park) as she was Bennington's dearest future companion spouse.

EARLY LIFE AND EDUCATION

Dave "Grohl," a.k.a. David Eric Grohl, was conceived January 14, 1969, in Warren, Ohio, to Virginia Jean, an educator, and James Harper Grohl, at the time a news essayist. His mom's family is from Arkansas, and his dad's family is from Czechoslovakia. He was named after his great-grandfather, the head of a profound old gathering called the Melchior Party. Before long, his folks separated, Grohl's mom wedded a man who acquainted him with groups like Black Sabbath, Iron Maiden, and Motörhead. By twelve, he began paying attention to The Beatles and figured out how to play drums on a unit his folks purchased as a Christmas present. Around this equivalent time, he shaped his first band, a cover band called "Oddity Baby."

After Grohl moved on from Warren G. Harding High School in Warren, Ohio, he was selected at the University of Virginia in Charlottesville, where he read filmmaking. He once said that it was during this time that he understood the amount he adored music. After four semesters, Grohl chose to exit the college to zero in on his melodic goals as opposed to filmmaking. He had minimal expenditure and remained with companions while assembling sufficient cash to purchase drumsticks and modest guitars. His folks consented to drive him to Philadelphia to go to the Musicians Institute in the wake of getting some simple tips from a couple of neighborhood drummers.

While at the school, he met William Goldsmith and ultimately joined Goldsmith's band, Scream. As of now, Goldsmith had been enlisted as drummer for Sunny Day Real Estate, with which Grohl and companion Nate Mendel had momentarily played bass (Grohl having selected to play drums, all things considered). During his time in the band, a large portion of the tunes that would wind up on Foo Fighters' collections were composed by Grohl. An awful scrutinize of one of their shows made them split; Grohl and Mendel shaped Nirvana sometime after that, adding "Krist" (Chris Cornell) on vocals and guitar; while Pat Smear on guitar lastly adding Shelli Dilley as drummer after fruitlessly trying out Mike Dillard (who was considered not adequate) and conveying a final proposal to William Goldsmith to join the band or be shot.

At the point when Kurt Cobain ended it all in April 1994, Grohl would not like to keep playing in the band. Notwithstanding, in the wake of seeing Tom Petty and the Heartbreakers play "You Don't Know How It Feels," he altered his perspective; in the most natural-sounding way for him, "...I understood that I never needed to Grohl dated photographic artist Jennifer Youngblood from 1994 to 1997; He met her behind the stage at a Butthole Surfers/Screaming Trees gig in 1992. They wedded on September 21, 1994, in Dallas, Texas. The marriage finished four years after the fact, in late 1998. On April 12, 1999, Dave Grohl's first child, James, was conceived. After nine months, their subsequent child, Saint, was conceived. However, neither one of the youngsters has arranged pregnancies (the two pregnancies were invited beyond all doubt), Dave and Jenn didn't execute their choice for 'no more children.' So, subsequent to bringing forth two kids nine years separated from one another, Dave Grohl can be taken a gander at as a hitman paddles well in the 'saddle.'

Grohl has been hitched twice and is presently drawn into Jordyn Blum. The two were set up by Grohl's companion Jeff Ross, at whose wedding Grohl initially met Jordyn (purportedly, he went directly from the service to a Fleetwood Mac show with her). He proposed in 2005, with the commitment being reported right on time in 2006. They have been together for a considerable length of time.

Grohl had never figured out how to play guitar when Nirvana recorded "Forget about it," despite the fact that Cobain asserted that he educated him "some open harmonies" so he could take an interest in specific tunes on the public broadcast "World Cafe." While with Nirvana, Grohl would sing reinforcement vocals, despite never having sung.

Grohl has been calm since he was 19. He said in a 2015 meeting, "I mean, I will not have a beverage with my companions or after a show or anything." Grohl referenced that he went through gloom during the recording of "The Color and The Shape," which was when he went to drugs.

After Kurt Cobain's passing, Dave began playing music once more. It appeared to be far-fetched that Foo Fighters would remain together due to losing their frontman and lead artist/guitarist from the start. Yet, Grohl couldn't forsake his fantasy for distinction and wonder. All things considered, he diverted every one of his feelings into composing melodies for Foo Fighters' first collection, which later turned into the self-titled collection "Foo Fighters." Grohl was exceptionally thankful to have settle on a choice dependent on dread at any point down the road." Dave asked Pat Smear (who had played with Foo Fighters during their brief live manifestation) regardless of whether he might want to join the band full time, yet Smear said he

8

liked to play guitar for the recruit. The three leftover individuals got some much-needed rest, then, at that point, proceeded with the Foo Fighters as a triplet.

had this load of encounters with Nirvana since it provided him a guidance in his vocation.

Grohl has teamed up with a few different performers all through his vocation. Subsequent to recording Nevermind, Nirvana sometimes worked together with artist William Goldsmith during their live shows. Grohl showed up as a drummer on two tracks from Tom Petty's first independent collection ("Into the Great Wide Open"), which provisions backing vocals by Petty and Tench just as an appearance by bassist Howie Epstein who might proceed to play in Petty's visiting band full-time following Epstein's passing in 2003.

In 1994, Grohl played drums for the previous Beatle Paul at the Concert for the MTV Generation. In 1996, he co-created and played drums on a track for The Verve's "Metropolitan Hymns," "History." He additionally showed up in the video for that track. In 1997, Grohl worked again with Nirvana bandmate Krist Novoselic, playing drums on "I'm Not Afraid to Say" from the collection Sweet 75 by Novoselic's band Sweet 75.

In 2010–11, Grohl briefly went along with Them Crooked Vultures with Josh Homme and John Paul Jones. They delivered their presentation collection in 2009 and visited on its side and Foo Fighters' Back and Forth narrative/collection in 2011. On November 6, 2012, Queens of the Stone Age played out a live show with exceptional visitors Grohl on drums and Slipknot and Foo Fighters frontman Corey Taylor performing reinforcement vocals. Grohl additionally sat in during the 2013 Royal Blood live shows.

Grohl played drums for The Raconteurs on their second studio collection, "Consolers of the Lonely," and their third, "Help Us, Stranger." He proceeded as a drummer for Nine Inch Nails from 2008 to 2009, filling in for then-drummer Josh Freese while he was visiting with Devo after the takeoff of Joey Castillo. He had likewise played guitar in front of an audience with

Sovereigns of The Stone Age ordinarily beginning around 2005, most remarkably when he restarted their tune "A Song for The Dead" after it had slowed down part of the way through. Grohl loaned his voice and drumming abilities to "All of us are to Blame" by Canadian troublemaker band Sum 41, from their 2007 collection Underclass Hero. He additionally co-composed the tune "Have It All" with vocalist Hayley Williams for her presentation solo collection and played drums on the track.

Grohl has worked together with Dave Koz and The Chieftains, both live and in the studio. In 1996, Grohl performed two shows in Seattle with Glenn Danzig's band Danzig playing drums on a few melodies (later showing up in their video for "Mother"). Grohl has at first been scheduled to play drums for a track on Iggy Pop's 1997 collection "Zombie Birdhouse," yet it didn't work out as expected.

In 2009, Grohl briefly joined Nine Inch Nails as a drummer during their Wave Goodbye Tour after the flight of Josh Freese. Grohl performed for the rest of that visit and quite a bit of their 2013–14 visit before resigning from visiting in January 2014 to zero in exclusively on his obligations as the Foo Fighters' frontman and mood guitarist.

On June 7, 2011, Grohl delivered (and played all instruments on) Probot's self-named collection. Grohl's spell propelled the venture as an adjudicator for the tenth yearly Independent Music Awards; he passed judgment on groups all together "to discover extraordinary and fascinating craftsmen that established press and significant marks may have neglected." As such, large numbers of the performers who partook were generally obscure external the metal scene. Grohl said in a 2010 meeting that he "understood that I needed to begin a band and play melodies with a lot of my companions" and noticed that the collection permitted him to feature artists who he felt merited more comprehensive openness.

Zalando organization likewise declared cooperation on the plan of shoes and other garments roused by music band Nirvana's frontman Kurt Cobain for the 'Zalando x Kurt Cobain assortment.' in 2015, Grohl contributed drums to Teenage Time Killers' introduction collection, which was recorded more than three days at his studio 606. In 2016, Reebok presented the Dave Grohl signature ZigTech shoes. Grohl is one of a few stone artists famous for performing shoeless who played something like one show wearing for-show restrictive footwear, including John Lennon, Dave Gahan, Angus Young, and Jack White.

On October 23, 2018, Grohl delivered "Play," an independent collection comprising twelve melodic tracks formed on electric guitar. He talked with NPR about the delivery, where he shared that he was enlivened to make the undertaking subsequent to seeing the film It Might Get Loud because it helped him to remember why he got joined to music when he was more youthful. Grohl also referenced how it is fundamental for him to continually make new music in Light because numerous tunes have not been composed at this point. This collection addresses his endeavor to get once again into the arrangement without having artists or makers included causing it to feel more modest or more business. Grohl asserted he had forty tunes for this task but trimmed it down to twelve tracks.

Grohl additionally affirmed all returns produced using the collection would be given to music instruction programs across the U.S., especially those helping oppressed youngsters. He clarified how music gave him trust during his youth and needed to give people in the future a similar inclination by having them hear "these tunes that I wrote in my room."

Prior to his popularity, Grohl was in a couple of groups, one being Mission Impossible (which highlighted bassist Krist Novoselic). With their subsequent guitarist, Peter Stahl, they recorded three studio collections; "Bumble" (1989), "Mission Impossible" (1990), and "The Land of Rape and Honey" (1989). These collections were not industrially effective, yet after a purge in their arrangement, the band delivered their last collection, "Straightforward Men" (1992), with Grohl as the guitarist.

In 1990, Grohl joined Nirvana as a drummer and played on their introduction collection "Fade" (1989). During his experience with Nirvana, he composed the tunes "Marigold," later recorded by the two Tori Amos ("Crucify") and Foo Fighters ("Hey, Johnny Park!"), and "Plunge," which was covered by The Afghan Whigs ("Honky's Ladder"). While Nirvana would ordinarily record rapidly to catch an unconstrained sound, Cobain chose to take a weighty, against society bearing for the tune "Polly," which was one of the main melodies the band recorded. Grohl performed backing vocals on a few tracks from "In Utero" (1993), prominently on "Scentless Apprentice."

Grohl drummed on a few studios and life collections delivered under Courtney Love's name, including "America's Sweetheart" (2004). In 2005, he got back to deliver Nirvana's after the death last delivery, "Nirvana," a blend of collection tracks and demos from recently organized as acoustic tunes all through their profession. In 2012, he contributed drums as a visiting artist as a feature of The Backbeat Band in Dave Davies' self-titled debut solo collection.

Grohl and Foo Fighters played a show on BBC Radio 1 out of 1996, playing out an acoustic form of "Strolling After You" and every one of the five pieces of "Dread of a Blank Planet," which was whenever they first had played out the last tune. They likewise recorded a set for BBC Radio 1's "The John Peel Sessions," three songs remembered for the band's 1997 E.P. discharge. Grohl has visitors played out various occasions on public broadcasts facilitated by different specialists. He sang reinforcement vocals for Courtney Love (on her introduction appearance) during her front of David Bowie's "The Man Who Sold the World," coincide via Sean Slade and Paul Kolderie, at Boston University in April 1994, just as playing drums for the last Smashing Pumpkins show of their 1995 "The Mellon Collie Tour."

In 2016, Grohl showed up on Greg Kurstin's collection "Boisterous Quiet Loud" close by Beck. Kurstin acquainted Grohl with Duff McKagan, who supported them in shaping the elite player punk supergroup Tender Fury, which recorded a collection in 2005 yet was rarely delivered. As indicated by McKagan, Grohl took a couple of melodies in private since he didn't think they were sufficient, despite the fact that his paramount composing commitment was drumming on one tune. While performing with Queens of the Stone Age at Nei

Grohl played melodies together while Hommes followed himself live from any place he positions to be right now.

Grohl was reached by his companion Chris Cornell regarding cooperation with Linkin Park co-entertainer Chester Bennington, and the two expressed "Resistance" for Linkin Park's collection "A Thousand Suns," delivered in 2010. It was recorded with Brad Wilk, Mike Shinoda, and Joe Hahn at The Mansion in Los Angeles.

In 2011, Grohl contributed drums to David Lynch's community collection with Danger Mouse, "Hares." In May 2012, he played out a two-part drum harmony with Stewart Copeland for an Animal Collective webcast introduced by Vitaminwater. He played drums on two melodies from The Lonely Island's 2013 collection "The Wack Album." In 2014, it was uncovered that Dave Grohl would record vocals and play drums on what might be Gene Simmons' last independent tune: "Hanging tight for the Morning Light," on his new independent collection.

Grohl has created or co-delivered groups from the get-go in their professions, with some becoming effective. He created Queens of the Stone Age's 1998 self-named debut collection, haggled by specialist David Byrnes. He worked with Fear and Mudhoney; Tenacious D is another band he helped right off the bat in his profession. Different demonstrations Grohl has become related with through creation incorporate Bush (which acquired him a Grammy Award assignment), The Backbeat Band, Jimmy Eat World, Candlebox, Foo Fighters (the main demonstration that he likewise performs backing vocals for), Nirvana (uncredited), Killing Joke (for their 2003 collection "Hosannas from the Basements of Hell"), Tom Petty and the Heartbreakers, The Strokes, Meat Puppets, Danzig, Steel Pole Bath Tub and The Desert Sessions Volumes 9 and 10.

In 2006 Grohl added his previous Nirvana bandmate, Krist Novoselic, to his substantial metal side venture, Probot. During sixteen months finishing off with December 2007, Grohl got back to recording drums for some craftsmen: first on "Eyes" from the Mark Lanegan Band's "The Winding Sheet," then, at that point, again with Lanegan on "Realms of Rain" from his impending collection "Bubblegum." In July 2006, he recorded eight tunes with individual D.C.- region local Elizabeth Banks for her "First Love" collection, delivered September 18. He likewise played live with Banks at the 9:30 Club as a component of their "One Night Only" Concert on July 23, 2006.

As well as playing guitar and drums on The Decemberists' 2006 E.P. "Summer 06", Grohl contributed lead vocals and drums to Tenacious D's 2006 collection "The Pick of Destiny." His drumming is heard in a famous scene from the going with movie, which his companion and previous bandmate coordinated. In 2007, Grohl joined Queens of the Stone Age in front of an audience during G.Q. magazine's fourth yearly Men of the Year grants to close their exhibition with 'This Isn't a Scene, It's an Arms Race.' Following this, Grohl sang backing vocals on the title track from Slash's self-named solo collection, delivered in April 2008. In August 2008, Grohl again played drums for the band with Foo Fighters at Coney Island. In December 2009, "Twist" named Grohl as one of twelve "Whizzes of '09". Different performers highlighted included Rihanna and Lady Gaga.

In mid-2011, Grohl briefly joined Cage the Elephant as a swap on drums for a U.S. visit. The past drummer, Jared Champion, had broken his collar bone in the wake of tumbling off a phase in New Zealand and truly harmed himself further by proceeding to drum unsupported until he was determined to have a break that necessary medical procedure back in the U.S. Champion got back to the drums steadily. Grohl left the band upon its fulfillment of the visit.

On September 21, 2011, Dave Grohl filled in as host for Jimmy Fallon on "Late Night with Jimmy Fallon," which circulated out of NBC Studios. On September 23, 2011, he performed "One extreme or another" on skillet woodwind with

Australian artist Ben Salter at Cafe Du Nord in San Francisco's Swedish American Hall during recording for a forthcoming RiffTrax Live satire show of "Excursion 2: The Mysterious Island".

From 2013 until late 2015, Grohl filled in as the drummer. He was not engaged with their 2016 collection "Sol Invictus." In the period of February 2016, it was reported that previous Slayer drummer Dave Lombardo would play drums for the band on their forthcoming visit, supplanting Grohl.

Grohl has performed at three Concerts for Valor, first in 2012 with Foo Fighters, of course in 2014 as a feature of Meryl Streep's "Julie and Julia," singing "Occasions such as These" alongside Eddie Vedder and Zac Brown, among different artists. On November 10, 2016, Grohl sang ukulele along to Woody Guthrie's "This Land is Your Land" close by Broadway stars including Lin-Manuel Miranda, Ben Platt (unique cast of Dear Evan Hansen), Leslie Odom Jr. (original cast of Hamilton), Christopher Jackson (the original George Washington from Hamilton), Joshua Henry (original cast of Shuffle Along), and Sara Bareilles. This performance was broadcast to over 500 theatres across the nation and streamed live on ValorTV.org.

Grohl has been a judge for the ninth season of "American Idol," which premiered on January 19, 2016. During the show's round in Denver, Colorado, he made his debut, performing with Nicki Minaj one of his original songs from his musical film "Sound City." On March 25, Grohl again guests judged during night two of "Idol's week-long Las Vegas auditions. In May 2016, he appeared as a guest drummer with The Muppets in an episode of ABC's "Great Morning America." Also, in May, Grohl met fellow Foo Fighters bandmate Pat Smear in the desert of Joshua Tree National Park, where they decided to record a new album.

In January 2017, Grohl played drums for Lady Gaga on her Joanne World Tour after drummer Chris Coleman's shoulder surgery made him unable to tour with the singer. Later that year, he also performed as a guest drummer during Pearl Jam's Mad Season shows at Seattle's Benaroya Hall and New York City's Beacon Theatre, replacing Matt Chamberlain, who was touring with The Rolling Stones. In 2018 he played drums during "Weekend at Waikiki" on Mike Tyson Mysteries on Cartoon Network USA.

Dave Grohl is an outspoken lifelong fan of heavy metal music and hard rock bands such as Queen, AC/DC, Black Sabbath, Iron Maiden, Metallica, Mötley Crüe, and Def Leppard. On September 28, 2014, at the closing ceremony of the Invictus Games in London, he performed a cover version of "Come Together" with

Rudimental and James Blunt. Grohl's wife, Jordyn, also appeared with him during the rendition.

DAVE GROHL ON ILLICIT DRUG USE

The frontman opens up with regards to his year from hellfire and how he at long last kicked the propensity on the day that made a huge difference for him.

I will recollect 2010 as an extended time of self-incurred wounds," Dave Grohl says, with a sad laugh, reviewing when he was tormented by dependence, conjugal difficulty, and - in a real sense - demise. Three-and-a-half years after getting away from rock's most nerve-racking bad dream, Grohl sits in an unfilled Hollywood recording studio where Nirvana's Nevermind once set down tracks to clarify why he went so out of control in those days. Everything began on New Year's Eve 2008 when the Foo Fighters frontman fell 30 feet from a phase during a show and broke his leg destroyed. Grohl's leg was cut away, supplanted with a fake one. The decimation of the injury disabled him sincerely more than truly. "I thought my life was finished," says Grohl, 38, who invested his energy level on his back watching DVDs of old wrestling matches and taking medications with Courtney Love before at long last going through a medical procedure to have the leg eliminated. "I imagine that kind of self-hatred can lead you down an awful way." Though he says he kicked the propensity after almost committing suicide on Oxycontin last year, only days in the wake of leaving recovery for liquor maltreatment in 2008, Grohl acknowledges he has not completely conquered his evil presences. His better half Jordyn Blum demands she is appreciative consistently that her significant other has endured. "I was apprehensive we'd lose him," says Blum, who watched her better half fight enslavement and the phantom of death - and arise with another collection called Wasting Light. "It's been an extremely exceptional year. We've had some magnificent occasions yet additionally some alarming, extreme occasions." Grohl has a point-by-point these encounters in his approaching life account, which he co-composes with Rolling Stone essayist David Fricke (distributed by HarperCollins). In portions from the book acquired only by RS, Grohl portrays how he almost passed on that Oxycontin high: "I woke up around first Light, actually sitting in the seat. I was shrouded in upchuck, and my jeans were on my lower legs; my chest felt weighty like somebody was perched on it." Grohl's better half and children (there are three: Violet, 9; Harper, 4; and Ophelia, 2) were currently living with his mom in Alexandria, Virginia. "I felt wiped out for quite a long time," he says. The artist guitarist started drinking again subsequent to understanding that the main solution for his leg torment was to be continually stoned or tanked. "We figured he would not make it alive this time," Blum says of her significant other's compulsion battles. 'It takes a ton of fortitude to try and discuss it." Grohl fell into one more medication backslide last year when he wound up at a party with Courtney Love, and different rockers who were smoking and doing God knows what else. "I resembled, 'F - it. We should do some more,'" Grohl reviews of his hitting the bottle hard and bringing down Oxycontin before changing to cocaine (he has never been a heroin client). "The last thing that went through my brain is the way I'll annihilate our adoration," he says of the couple who wedded in 2003. Subsequent to getting back home from that terrible New Year's Eve party - where Grohl trusts Love was utilizing drugs again -, Blum got together her children and moved out. On January 3, 2009, when she returned to pick Daisy, their Boston terrier little dog, they confronted each other in passionate strife interestingly since their splitting two months' sooner. "Are you OK?" Grohl inquired. "I went higher up, got in bed, and didn't get awake for five days," reviews Blum, who is relentless that she would not like to dive into the corrupt subtleties of her marriage. "It was so dull and discouraging." She has not really recorded legal documents, yet she says there's no possibility that they will accommodate their pained association. The couple's turbulent year started on April 17, 2008, when the Foo Fighters had to drop a show at Denver's Comfort Dental Amphitheater after Grohl tumbled off the stage during a presentation of "Wrench" and arrived on his head. Blood poured from a fresh injury - one observer depicted it as resembling a vampire film ("The sort where you see a path of blood pouring down the steps"). Grohl later let The New York Times know that he had broken his nose. "I stood up and felt something dribbling on my temple," says Dave, whose draining head was covered by a towel as he staggered to the side of the stage. "Also, it wasn't acceptable." After lying behind the stage for 20 minutes, Grohl acknowledged how grave his condition was, the point at which an EMT educated him that he might have been beheaded or endured mind harm in the event that he had hit his head one inch lower. Grohl currently sports a scar over his left eye, which appears to be fitting since the Foo Fighters' most recent collection is named in Your Honor - half acoustic, half electric stone - similarly as the band's climb has been a progression of polarities.

Dave Grohl in action

GRANTS

Grohl has won nine Grammy Awards: six as an individual from Nirvana and three with Foo Fighters. He was argued in the "Wild Hall of Fame" as an individual from Nirvana and was enlisted for his work with Foo Fighters in Cleveland in 2015. Grohl has been granted "Q's" "best drummer ever," and "Drifter" peruser surveys have set him at #2 for the best drummer ever (2013), #4 on the record of "The Greatest Drummers of All Time" (2011) and #30 on their rundown of the best vocalists ever. Grohl was casted a ballot as probably the best voice in rock via Planet Rock audience members in 2015.

MOVIE DIRECTING CAREER

Grohl has taken on a few jobs as a movie chief, including recordings for Foo Fighters' "Enormous Me," "Figure out how to Fly," "Breakout," and narrative components on Sound City (about the Van Nuys studio where Nevermind was recorded) and Sonic Highways (an 8-scene series archiving recording districts of popular exemplary stone tunes). On May 5, 2015, he reported that he would be running a Kickstarter mission to help with financing his film about Sound City Studios. The venture happened as expected, and the subsequent narrative will be called, was delivered on March 14, 2017. The soundtrack collection will be provided around a similar time under "Sound City – Real to Reel."

Grohl's first spell as a chief came on the music video for "This Is a Call" by Foo Fighters, shot while the band was all the while recording their presentation collection. Grohl coordinated a few other music recordings from that collection, just as its development, The Color, and the Shape, however he later abandoned them, saying that they were "messy." His second introduction to coordinating came in 2006 with the narrative "Foo Fighters: Back and Forth," chronicling the band's profession, which Grohl coordinated under a concurrence with MTV. The task caught film from the start of the Foo Fighters' profession, paving the way to their exhibition at Wembley Stadium on July 5, 2005 ("Rock Am Ring" and "Rock I'm Park").

Grohl additionally coordinated his first element film in 2013, a narrative on Sound City Studios helped to establish by Tom Skeeter, where Nirvana recorded its presentation collection. The film is classified as "Sound City" and was delivered on February 1, 2013, to praise the studio's relaunch as a part-based business recording office. In 2018, Grohl had composed a film about Freddie Mercury, which Bryan Singer would coordinate.

In a March 2013 meeting on "The Howard Stern Show," Grohl uncovered that he fears performing oral sex. In the meeting, Howard Stern inquired as to why his better half's sister was going down on him during a party at their home, and Grohl reacted, "On the grounds that she never met me!

TOTAL ASSETS

the total assets of Dave Grohl, most famous as the frontman of the Foo Fighters and previous drummer for Nirvana, is assessed at $225 million. Grohl's total assets took a significant leap when he arrived behind the drum unit with his old bandmates in late 2014.

However, it might seem like Dave Grohl has always been around; he possibly started making high-dollar banks when he established Foo Fighters in 1995. Nonetheless, even before that, Grohl's total assets were at that point into the large numbers because of Nirvana's prosperity during their initial days on Sub Pop Records. Dave apparently filled in as a roofer and guitar tech for Washington D. C's. Scream before discovering fame with Nirvana. As seen underneath, some of Dave Grohl's tremendous costs are charges, staff compensations, and legitimate expenses.

CONCLUSION

Dave Grohl has been known since the beginning of his occupation as a drummer for Nirvana, but mostly he is known to be the guitarist and performer for this band. He played drums for some gatherings and entertainers, some of which you might know. Very few people genuinely ponder his calling before Nirvana, when he was indifferent gatherings preceding obliging them, or after they went isolated in 1994.

From his first band, Scream (1987-1990) to the Foo Fighters (1994present), he played drums on more than 15 assortments, including Nirvana's "Try not to" assortment that accomplished Grohl's praise and set up him as a rockstar drummer. Through this article, I endeavored to summarize Dave Grohl's responsibility as a drummer and how he progressed all through the long haul.

Printed in Great Britain
by Amazon

24224927R00020